MW00983365

Tom Tierney

Phillis Wheatley

do not cut
out white area
between left arm
and body

PLATE 1

Tom Tierney

Sojourner Truth

PLATE 2

Pauline Cushman

PLATE 3

"Madam" C. J. Walker

PLATE 4

do not cut
out white areas
between arms
and body

Tom Tierney

Mary McLeod Bethune

PLATE 5

do not cut
out white areas
between arms
and body

Zora Neale Hurston

PLATE 6

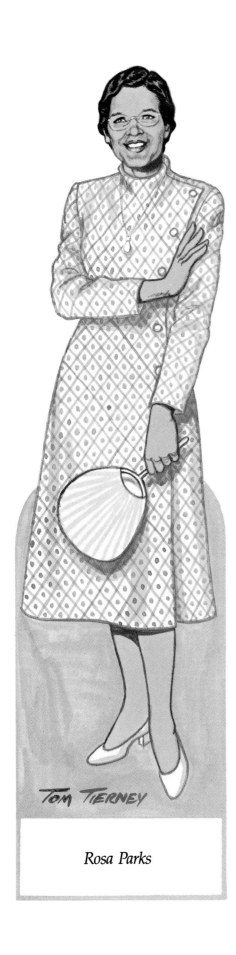

Rosa Parks

PLATE 7

do not cut
out white area
between left arm
and body

Tom Tierney

Patricia Roberts Harris

PLATE 8

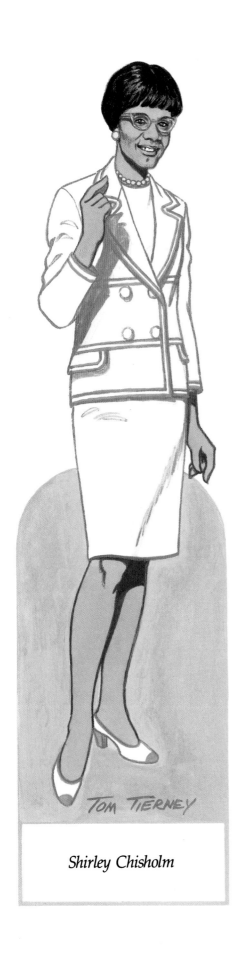

Shirley Chisholm

PLATE 9

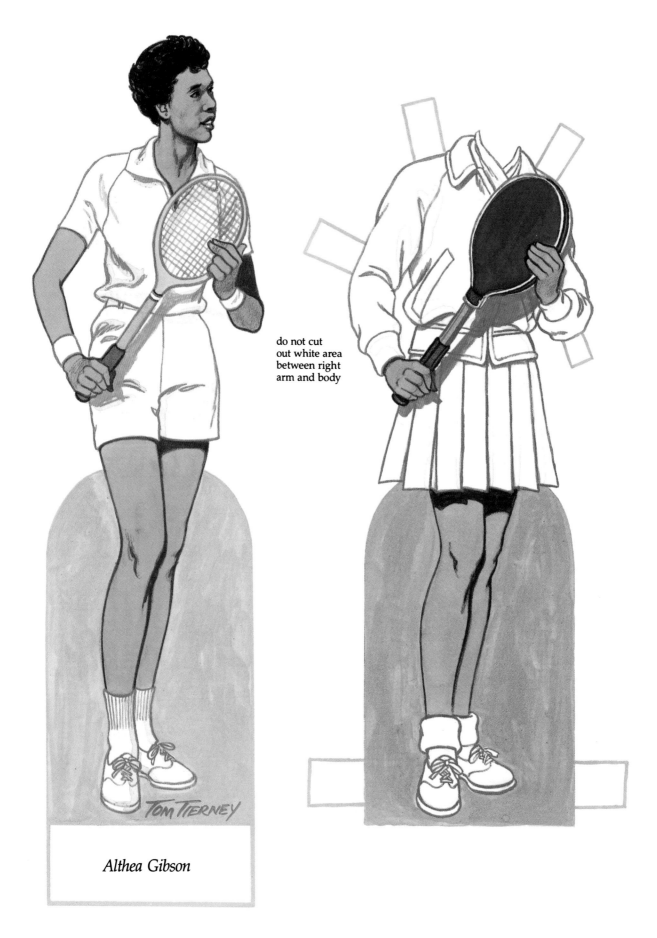

do not cut
out white area
between right
arm and body

Althea Gibson

PLATE 10

Leontyne Price

Tom Tierney

PLATE 11

TOM TIERNEY

Maya Angelou

PLATE 12

Toni Morrison

PLATE 13

Barbara Jordan

Tom Tierney

PLATE 14

do not cut
out white area
between left arm
and body

Judith Jamison

PLATE 15

Mae C. Jemison, M.D.

PLATE 16